Cooking with Cranberries

Lura Rogers

CONTENTS

The American Cranberry..2

   Cranberry Production..2

   Selecting and Storing Cranberries................................3

   Cranberries and Health 4

Cranberries Make the Meal....................................5

Drinks, Sauces, and Sides.......................................14

Sweets and Treats..22

Resources 32

The American Cranberry
Vaccinium marocarpon

Early European settlers in North America learned about the cranberry from Native Americans, who valued the berry both as food and for its medicinal qualities. The cranberry was considered a symbol of peace by some native cultures, including the tribe later known as the Delaware Indians. The name of the berry varied by region. The Cape Cod Pequots called it *ibimi*, which means "bitter berry"; it was also called *sassamanesh* in the East and *atoqua* in Algonquin country. Strangely, today's name came not from one of these original words but from a word created by European settlers. When they were introduced to the plant, its flower reminded them of the head of a crane, and they called the fruit a "crane-berry."

For Native Americans, the cranberry had important, and varied, uses. The bright berry was a popular source of red dye for cloth of all types. It was applied to wounds to help draw out poison. When it was discovered that something (enzymes, we now know) in the cranberry preserved meat for many days — an esteemed quality for a berry in the era before refrigeration! — cranberries were mixed with venison to make pemmican.

Cranberry Production

In their native habitat of North America, cranberries are grown in Massachusetts, Wisconsin, New Jersey, British Columbia, Nova Scotia, and Oregon. At one time, the Cape Cod area of Massachusetts was the leading cranberry producer, but now Wisconsin leads, producing more than half of North America's cranberry crop, according to the Cranberry Institute (see Resources). Cranberries grow naturally in wild bogs, but these bogs can't grow cranberries for mass consumption because of their varying sizes, shapes, and terrain and their irregular flooding patterns. The commercial cranberry bog is a naturally occurring bog that has been prepared for production. The ideal bog is level and has a dependable source of water for flooding, but also drains easily.

Cranberry crops are generally not ready for harvest until 3 to 6 years after planting. As a cranberry plant's root structure increases, the plant grows runners and branches, both of which grow bright green leaves that turn red in winter. In late June, the branches begin to flower, and by October, the fruit has ripened. Only branches, not runners, produce berries. Once the berries have turned the characteristic bright red, they are ready to be harvested.

There are two methods of harvest: dry and wet. The dry method is used to collect the cranberries we buy fresh from the grocery store. These cranberries are collected with a large rake picker attached to a helicopter; harvesting from above keeps the fragile bogs and vines from being crushed. Some smaller, organic farms pick their berries by hand.

The wet method is used to harvest those berries typically used for juices and other processed cranberry products. In this method, a bog is flooded for at least 12 hours before large, beaterlike machines whisk through it, knocking the berries off the vines. The berries float to the top of the water (about 1 foot [30 cm] above the plants) and are skimmed into containers and trucked to a processing center. The bog is flooded for about 2 years after it has been cleared of cranberry plants.

Selecting and Storing Cranberries

Cranberries are among the simplest fruits to judge and keep. A bright red berry is a fresh berry, packed with flavor. Beware of any berries with wrinkly skins or squishy bodies. The fresher the berry, the more time you'll have to think up new ways to eat it! Size is not a prerequisite for a good berry. I have found many a little berry that has packed a mighty punch while its big brother lumbered lazily along.

In most areas, shoppers can choose to buy organic produce. Organic cranberry crops are grown without pesticides or fertilizers. They yield fewer berries per year at a higher price. The cost to consumers is slightly greater, but so is the fruit's wholesomeness, an important consideration for many.

Whole cranberries usually keep for several weeks in the refrigerator; in the freezer, they last at least 9 months. Whole frozen cranberries can be substituted for fresh in many recipes, and older frozen berries may be used in recipes that require you to cook the berries. Do be aware, however, of the differences among store-bought varieties of frozen cranberries — some are presweetened and cut, and this variety will not work well in many recipes.

Sweetened dehydrated cranberries and canned jellies and sauces are readily available in supermarkets. Cranberry juices are found in a plethora of forms, including unsweetened concentrates, ready-to-mix concentrates, juice blends, organic juices, and more. Cranberries can even be found in pill form in the supplement section of health food stores.

Cranberries and Health

The cranberry is the focus of quite a bit of medical research. You may have heard about the cranberry's ability to improve urinary tract health, but did you know that cranberries have been used to relieve symptoms of urinary tract infection since at least colonial times? More recently, several studies at leading universities have concluded that the proanthocyanidin compounds present in the cranberry prevent offending bacteria from adhering to the walls of the bladder and urinary tract.

The cranberry has other bacteria- and fungi-fighting properties that are still being researched, including those that inhibit growth of *Candida, E. coli,* and *Staphylococcus* bacteria. Researchers have discovered that cranberry consumption may prevent and possibly reverse gum disease and stomach ulcers. (Although we think of the acidic cranberry as an ulcer's worst nightmare, it is actually bacteria that perpetuates most ulcers.)

And there's more! Along with other popular antioxidant fruits, such as blueberries, apples, and grapes, our little red friends have recently been found to contain large quantities of phenols, which prevent cellular oxidation. This makes the cranberry a cancer-fighting agent, thanks to a high percentage of flavonoids (these include anthocyanins, which give the cranberry its festive red). Also, the cranberry's antioxidant properties make it a hero for heart health, reducing atherosclerosis by preventing oxidation of cholesterol in the bloodstream.

See Resources on page 32 to find out where you can learn more about cranberries.

Cranberries Make the Meal

Whether eaten for breakfast, lunch, or dinner, cranberries make the meal. The little berries provide big flavor in everything from pancakes to pork chops. In fact, there are few dishes a healthy dose of cranberries couldn't improve! This chapter offers a sampling of my favorites.

COUNTRY INN GRANOLA

The currants in this recipe are made from dried Zante grapes, native to Greece. They are quite different from the tiny berry called a currant.

10 cups rolled oats (not instant oatmeal)
¼ cup pure Vermont maple syrup
¾ cup dried blueberries
¾ cup dried cranberries
½ cup dried apples, chopped
½ cup slivered almonds
½ cup Zante currants
½ cup chopped pecans
 1 tablespoon kosher salt
 1 cup granulated sugar
 1 cup light brown sugar, firmly packed
 1 cup apple cider or apple juice
¼ cup (½ stick) butter

1. In a large mixing bowl, combine the oats, syrup, blueberries, cranberries, apples, almonds, currants, pecans, and salt.

2. In a saucepan over low heat, dissolve the granulated and brown sugars in the cider and bring to a simmer. Continue simmering until the amount is reduced by one third, then add the butter in small pieces, stirring with a wire whisk.

3. Drizzle the cider syrup over the oat mixture, stirring well to prevent clumping.

4. Spread the mixture on a baking sheet and cool at room temperature for 30 minutes. Store in an airtight container, or freeze.

YIELD: 14–16 SERVINGS

CRANBERRY ANADAMA BREAD

The texture and character of the hearty Anadama bread cry out for the accent of a tart fruit, such as the cranberry. This bread is reminiscent of Native American recipes and uses the traditional cornmeal, which adds a warm touch to holiday meals and family gatherings. Anadama keeps well in the fridge or freezer, and it also makes incredible toast.

2½ cups water
⅔ cup stone-ground cornmeal
½ cup dark molasses
4 tablespoons (½ stick) butter
2½ teaspoons salt
2 envelopes active dry yeast
½ cup warm water (105–115°F)
¼ cup plus ½ teaspoon sugar
1½ cups fresh or frozen cranberries
Zest of 1 orange
7–8 cups all-purpose flour

1. Place the water in a large saucepan and bring to a boil.

2. Lower heat to medium-high and slowly add the cornmeal, stirring with a wire whisk. Cook until thickened, about 5 minutes, then add the molasses, butter, and salt. Set aside to cool.

3. While the cornmeal mush is cooling, dissolve the yeast in the warm water in a bowl and add ½ teaspoon of the sugar. Stir, then set aside. In a food processor, process the cranberries, the remaining ¼ cup sugar, and the orange zest for 30 seconds, just long enough to chop the berries and incorporate the sugar.

4. Once the cornmeal has cooled to room temperature (too much heat will kill the yeast and prevent the bread from rising), add the yeast and cranberry mixtures. Add flour gradually, until the dough becomes difficult to stir, then transfer to a well-floured counter.

5. Continue to knead in the remaining flour until the dough is smooth and elastic and bounces back when you poke it. Place in a lightly oiled glass bowl and cover with a dish towel. Move the bowl to a warm (not hot), draft-free place to rise for about 45 minutes, or until it doubles in bulk (on top of the refrigerator works well).

6. Grease two 9- x 5-inch loaf pans. Flour the counter again and turn out the dough, kneading it to press out the large air bubbles. Once

the dough is elastic, cut it in half with a sharp knife and place each half in a loaf pan. Cover with towels and allow to rise in the same draft-free space until the dough has reached the top of the pans, about 1 hour.

7. Preheat oven to 350°F. Bake for 45 minutes, or until the surfaces of the loaves are nicely browned. When you tap a loaf, it should sound hollow. Remove from pans to cool on a rack.

YIELD: 2 LOAVES

MORNING-AFTER PANCAKES

These hearty pancakes are convenient to make for breakfast the morning after Thanksgiving. They are also great as a side dish or a quick snack.

    2 cups leftover mashed potatoes
    ½ cup brown sugar
    ¼ cup sour cream
    3 eggs
    4 tablespoons all-purpose flour
    1 tablespoon baking powder
    ¾ cup fresh cranberries
    ¼ cup half-and-half or whole milk

1. Mix the potatoes, brown sugar, sour cream, and eggs in a bowl until blended.

2. In a separate bowl, mix the flour and baking powder. Add the cranberries and toss until they are thoroughly coated.

3. Pour the half-and-half into the potato batter and then add the cranberry mixture, stirring just to incorporate.

4. Lightly coat a cast-iron skillet with canola or corn oil. Heat on medium-high. Pour ¼-cup dollops of batter into the oil. Brown both sides and serve with your favorite syrup, maple cream, or leftover cranberry sauce.

YIELD: 12 PANCAKES

CRANBERRY–APPLE PANCAKES

A traditional family recipe, these pancakes were inspired by both my father and my grandmother. My father used to make these for me with the cranberries in the shape of a smiling face. We like these best with maple syrup or maple cream and butter.

 2 cups all-purpose flour
 2 tablespoons plus 2 teaspoons sugar
 2 tablespoons baking powder
 1 teaspoon salt
 4 eggs
1–1½ cups milk
 ½ cup fresh cranberries, halved
 ¼ teaspoon ground allspice
 ½ cup chopped Cortland apple

1. Mix the flour, 2 tablespoons of the sugar, the baking powder, and the salt. Whisk the eggs, then add to the flour mixture. Gradually add the milk until the batter has the consistency of a thick pudding.

2. In a separate bowl, toss the cranberries with the remaining 2 teaspoons of sugar. Add the allspice, toss, then add the apples and toss again.

3. Ladle the egg batter onto a hot greased skillet to make a pancake 4–5 inches in diameter. As soon as the batter has set, sprinkle a handful of the fruit mixture evenly into the pancake and cook until the surface of the pancake bubbles. Flip pancake and cook until firm and lightly browned.

YIELD: 12 PANCAKES

CREAM OF SWEET POTATO AND CRANBERRY SOUP

Wow guests with this simple soup's complex flavors. For flair, shape the cranberry purée into unique designs.

Cranberry Purée
   1½ cups fresh cranberries
   ½ cup port
   ¼ cup sugar
Sweet Potato Soup
   2 shallots, chopped
   1 carrot, thinly sliced
   ¼ cup (½ stick) butter
   3 cups chicken or turkey broth
   1½ pounds sweet potatoes, peeled and cut into 1-inch cubes
   ½ pound red potatoes, peeled and cut into 1-inch cubes
   ½ pound parsnips, peeled and cut into 1-inch cubes
   ¼ teaspoon ground ginger
   ¼ teaspoon ground mace
   ¼ teaspoon ground nutmeg
   ¼ teaspoon white pepper
   Kosher salt to taste

1. To prepare the cranberry purée, simmer the cranberries, port, and sugar over medium heat for 5–10 minutes, until the skins of the cranberries split and the liquid begins to thicken. Transfer to a blender or food processor and purée. Using a fine sieve and a spatula, remove the solids from the purée and discard them. Cover and refrigerate.

2. To make the soup, in a large pan, sauté the shallots and carrot in the butter until the vegetables are softened. Add 2 cups of the broth, the sweet and red potatoes, parsnips, ginger, mace, nutmeg, and white pepper. Cook, covered, over medium-low heat for 30 minutes. Test a few pieces of each vegetable to make sure all pieces are soft all the way through, then transfer to a blender or food processor to purée. Once all of the soup has been puréed, add the remaining 1 cup of broth gradually to desired consistency, then add the salt to taste and adjust the seasonings.

3. To serve, pour soup into bowls and pipe cranberry purée decoratively onto the soup's surface.

YIELD: 4–6 SERVINGS

FRUITED CHICKEN SALAD

Cranberries and chicken make a fine marriage. This dish is perfect for a summer picnic or a cool supper.

2 large chicken breasts, boned, cooked, and cubed (about 4 cups)
2 celery stalks, chopped (about ¾ cup)
1 can (11 ounces) mandarin oranges, drained
1 cup halved cranberries
¼ cup mayonnaise
3 tablespoons low-fat milk
   Juice of half a lemon
2 tablespoons finely chopped fresh parsley
2 teaspoons celery seed
2 teaspoons finely chopped fresh savory or
   1 teaspoon dried savory
   Salt
   Bibb lettuce

1. In a large bowl, combine the chicken, celery, oranges, and cranberries. Set aside.

2. Thin the mayonnaise with the milk and lemon juice. Add the parsley, celery seed, savory, and salt to taste. Mix well.

3. Combine the dressing with the chicken mixture and refrigerate. Serve cupped in leaves of Bibb lettuce.

YIELD: 6 SERVINGS

THE VERY BEST STUFFING

This recipe is very dear to me and my family. When I was 10 years old, my entire household disliked stuffing. Determined to have a stuffed bird like the other kids in school, I set out to make stuffing everyone would love. Now I have to make a triple batch! I begin preparing this well before the last-minute rush because the ingredients can all sit.

1½ cups dried cranberries
1 cup white rum
5 cups coarsely crumbled fresh corn bread (about 1½ loaves)
2 cups chopped pecans
4 stalks celery, chopped
2 Cortland apples, chopped
1 Vidalia onion, chopped
2 teaspoons dried marjoram
2 teaspoons freshly ground nutmeg
2 teaspoons dried sage
2 teaspoons dried thyme
½–1 cup chicken or turkey broth

1. Soak the dried cranberries in the rum for at least 3 hours.

2. In a very large mixing bowl, combine the corn bread, pecans, celery, apples, onion, marjoram, nutmeg, sage, and thyme. Add the cranberries and rum. About an hour and a half before the turkey is done, add ½ cup of the broth to the stuffing and mix well. If the stuffing is too dry, add more broth until it is slightly moist but not mushy. Spread the stuffing in a baking pan (a lasagne-type pan works well), cover tightly with aluminum foil, and place in the oven.

3. When the turkey has about 15 minutes left to cook, remove both it and the stuffing from the oven and scoop some stuffing into the turkey. (Be very careful when you take off the aluminum foil cover; there will be a good amount of steam built up!) Put the turkey back in the oven to finish off, and spread the rest of the stuffing evenly over the bottom of the baking pan. Return the pan to the oven, uncovered, until the turkey is done. If members of your family prefer a crispy stuffing, leave this in the oven while you carve, taking care to check it for signs of burning.

4. Serve the cooked-inside stuffing and the crispy pan-baked stuffing separately to offer different textures to suit individual tastes.

Yield: 8 cups

THANKSGIVING LEFTOVER MASH

Typically made with leftover turkey, this recipe is also delicious with left-over chicken or game hen. If you can't wait for a day with leftovers, grab an already-roasted bird from your grocery's deli counter. The potatoes, as well, should be precooked — keep this in mind a few nights in advance, and this will be a speedy meal to prepare. You'll find dried cranberries in the bulk foods section or the snack aisle of your supermarket.

1–2 tablespoons extra virgin olive oil
1 pound cooked, unpeeled mini-potatoes, quartered
1 pound cooked, diced turkey
1 cup dried cranberries
3 shallots, finely chopped
2 tablespoons fresh marjoram, chopped (may substitute
   2 teaspoons dried, crumbled)
⅓ cup sour cream
¼ cup half-and-half
½ teaspoon salt
Freshly ground black pepper

1. Heat a large cast-iron skillet on medium-high, then heat enough olive oil to amply coat the bottom of the pan. Add the potatoes and the turkey and toss with a sturdy pair of tongs. Add the cranberries, shallots, and marjoram and toss once more. Reduce heat to medium, and cover the pan.

2. Mix the sour cream and half-and-half in a small bowl until smooth. Add the salt and several coarse grinds of pepper and stir. Add the sour cream mixture to the potatoes and turkey and mix well.

3. Cover skillet and let sit for 5 minutes, then stir well. Cook, cov-ered, for another 10 minutes or so on medium heat, stirring occasion-ally, then uncover and raise heat to medium-high. Watch that the mash does not stick to the pan too much or get too dry. If it does, drop a tablespoon or two of olive oil onto a clear spot in the pan, let it heat up, and toss the mixture into the hot oil.

4. Cook, uncovered, at medium-high until crisp and browned, and stir frequently to prevent burning. Add salt and pepper to taste and serve hot.

YIELD: 4 SERVINGS

CRANBERRY PORK CHOPS

The ease of preparing these chops makes this scrumptious dish even more appealing!

6 pork chops
4 cups cranberries, chopped
1 medium onion, chopped
1 cup honey
Salt and freshly ground pepper

1. Preheat oven to 350°F.

2. In a large skillet, brown the pork chops on both sides over medium heat. Add salt and pepper to taste.

3. Combine the cranberries, onion, and honey in a bowl.

4. Place the pork chops in an ovenproof casserole dish. Spread the cranberry mixture over the pork chops, and cover. Bake for 1 hour.

YIELD: 6 SERVINGS

Drinks, Sauces, and Sides

From salsas to smoothies to spreads, the cranberry complements many savory sides. When you tire of cranberry juice cocktail, try some of these drink recipes. Fresh or frozen berries work fine, and you can use these recipes as a template for your own creations. Canning chutney, jelly, or preserves is a great way to preserve the berry — just remember to refrigerate after opening a sealed jar.

RED SNAPPER

This is my very favorite cocktail, created by a bartender named Victoria.

> **3 ounces cranberry juice cocktail**
> **1 jigger Amaretto di Saronno**
> **1 jigger Crown Royal**
> **1 slice orange, to garnish**

In a shaker, mix the cranberry juice, amaretto, and Crown Royal with crushed ice and pour into an old-fashioned glass. Garnish with the orange.

YIELD: 1 SERVING

CRANBERRY–PINEAPPLE SMOOTHIE

Relax outside with this yummy and cooling summer snack.

> **1½ cups plain yogurt**
> **1 cup crushed ice**
> **1 cup fresh ripe pineapple**
> **¾ cup fresh diced or frozen cranberries**
> **Juice of half a lemon**
> **Superfine sugar, to taste**

1. Place the yogurt, ice, pineapple, cranberries, and lemon juice in a blender and mix until the ice has been adequately blended. Add sugar until taste.

2. Divide into two glasses and insert straws.

Variations: You can replace the yogurt with the same amount of coconut milk or vanilla ice cream. Try serving with a scoop of ice cream floating in the glasses, or a slice of fresh fruit for garnish.

YIELD: 2 SERVINGS

MY FAVORITE FRUIT SMOOTHIE

Feel free to try different fruits to complement the cranberries in this traditional summer beverage. Ripe, chilled fruits are best, except for the banana, which should never be refrigerated.

    3 peaches
    ¾ cup fresh cranberries
    1 banana
    ¾ cup freshly squeezed orange juice
    ½ cup rice milk or milk
    3 scoops vanilla ice cream or substitute
      Maple syrup or superfine sugar

1. Place the peaches, cranberries, banana, orange juice, and rice milk in a blender and mix until smooth. Add the ice cream and blend.

2. Adjust consistency with more ice cream if the mixture is too thin; add milk if it's too thick.

3. Add maple syrup to taste.

YIELD: 2–3 SERVINGS

Fun Fruit Ideas for Smoothies

- **Apples** (slice them into orange juice to keep them from turning brown)
- **Apricots** (be sure to pit them!)
- **Cherries** (make sure they're ripe, sweet, and pitted)
- **Grapefruit** (balance this with a subtle sweetener, such as honey)
- **Kiwi** (you may need sweet fruit, maple syrup, or sugar to balance the tartness)
- **Mango**
- **Passion fruit** (balance quantities of ingredients carefully, because passion fruit's delicate flavor is easily overpowered)
- **Pears** (out of season, canned will do)
- **Strawberries** (frozen will work if partially thawed)
- **Watermelon**

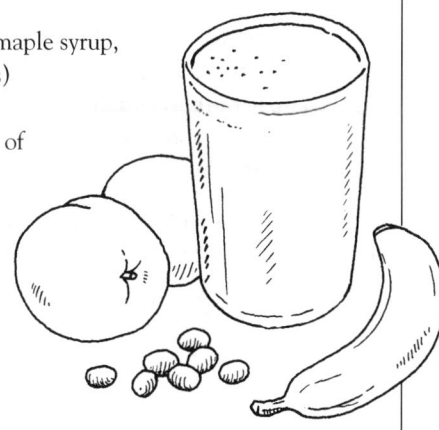

NON-DAIRY CRANBERRY SPRITZER

Are you lactose intolerant or just not in the mood for ice cream's calories? This great refresher is quick and easy, and very adaptable too.

¾ **cup fresh ripe or frozen cranberries**
3 **hulled strawberries**
1 **tablespoon mint, finely diced**
1 **liter ginger ale**
  Candied ginger, to garnish

1. Purée the cranberries, strawberries, mint, and ½ cup of the ginger ale in a blender until completely liquefied.

2. Distribute the mixture evenly into four glasses, and insert a long spoon in each.

3. Pour the ginger ale to 1 inch below the tops of the glasses and stir gently, then remove the spoons and insert straws in each glass. Garnish the edges of the glasses with scored pieces of candied ginger.

YIELD: 4 SERVINGS

ASIAN FUSION TEA

This cranberry-spiked tea is a sophisticated version of a favorite beverage my mother gave me when I had a head cold. She added orange juice to my tea and sent me off to a hot bath. But I suggest that you make this for yourself on a night when you feel well!

6 **tablespoons Gen-Mai Cha tea or other loose green tea**
3 **cups boiling water**
1½ **cups cranberry juice**
½ **cup pure maple syrup**
6 **tablespoons amaretto**

1. Brew the tea in the boiling water, covered, for 5–7 minutes. Add the cranberry juice and maple syrup and return to low heat to warm.

2. Pour 1 tablespoon of amaretto into each of six teacups, then pour in the cranberry tea. Serve with a smile.

YIELD: 6 SERVINGS

CRANBERRY COULIS

Serve this dish with grilled pork chops for a mouthwatering meal. And wear kitchen gloves when handling the chiles to keep the caustic juices away from your skin.

2 jalapeño chiles
2 tablespoons kosher salt
1 sweet red pepper
1 can (10 ounces) cranberry sauce
3 drops liquid smoke

1. Preheat the broiler. Place the jalapeños on a baking sheet. Broil evenly by turning frequently with tongs until the skins are black. Remove the jalapeños from the baking sheet and place them in a brown paper bag with the salt, shake a few times, then leave in the bag to steam.

2. Repeat this process with the red pepper, steaming it in the bag with the jalapeños.

3. Allow the red pepper and jalapeños to steam together for at least 10 minutes, then remove all peppers from the bag and run them under cold water, rubbing the skins off with your fingers. Seed the peppers and chop coarsely.

4. Place the cranberry sauce and liquid smoke in a blender, and begin to process. Add the pieces of pepper a few at a time, until all have been incorporated and liquefied. Store the coulis in the refrigerator for up to 1 week.

YIELD: 2 CUPS

CRANBERRY BUTTER

Cranberry butter is versatile and can be adapted to accommodate canned, frozen, or leftover cranberries. It is delicious spread on hot biscuits or as a filling in miniature tea sandwiches. Stir in some maple cream and serve as a topping for French toast or pancakes.

1 cup (2 sticks) butter or margarine, softened
2 tablespoons confectioners' sugar
⅓ cup cranberries, mashed

Mix all ingredients in a blender or food processor and blend until smooth. May be kept, refrigerated, for up to 2 weeks.

YIELD: 1¼ CUPS

CRANBERRY SALSA

Serve this salsa with blue corn chips, broiled salmon, pork chops, or game or mix a half cup with three mashed ripe avocados for a fun twist on guacamole. Wear kitchen gloves when handling the chiles.

2 cups fresh cranberries
1 medium Spanish onion, medium diced
3 tablespoons extra virgin olive oil
1 medium orange bell pepper
1 medium yellow bell pepper
1 tablespoon kosher salt
1 habanero chile, seeded and diced fine
1 jalapeño chile, seeded and diced fine
1 ripe peach, diced medium
2 fresh scallions, thinly sliced
4 tablespoons chopped fresh cilantro
2 tablespoons chopped fresh mint
3 tablespoons granulated sugar
Juice of 1 fresh lime

1. Preheat oven to 425°F.

2. Combine the cranberries and onion in a bowl with 2 tablespoons of the olive oil. Spread this mixture on a baking sheet and roast for 10 minutes or so, until the onions are slightly brown and the skins of the cranberries begin to split. Set aside to cool in a large mixing bowl.

3. Turn oven to broil.

4. Place the orange and yellow bell peppers on a baking sheet. Broil, turning with tongs regularly, until the skin of each pepper is black and blistered. Remove from the oven, place in a paper bag with the salt, and roll the top of the bag. Give it a good shake to distribute the salt and set aside to steam for 10 minutes.

5. While the bell peppers are steaming, add the habanero, jalapeño, peach, scallions, cilantro, mint, sugar, and lime juice to the bowl with the onions and cranberries. Mix well.

6. Remove the bell peppers from the paper bag and run under very cold water, rubbing with both hands. The blackened peels should come off easily. Halve the peppers, scoop out the seeds, and dice the peppers. Add diced peppers to the bowl and mix.

7. Scoop 1½ cups of the mixture into a food processor and purée until smooth. Stir the purée into the remaining mixture. Refrigerate the salsa for a minimum of 2 hours before serving.

YIELD: ABOUT 4 CUPS

ROGERS FAMILY CRANBERRY RELISH

We love this relish so much that we've created a tart so that we can enjoy it for dessert (see page 25). But we like it on its own, too!

- 1 **pound fresh cranberries**
- 1 **orange, quartered and seeded**
- ¾ **cup sugar**
- ¼ **teaspoon nutmeg**

1. Grind the cranberries and orange together in a food processor or food mill.

2. Stir in the sugar and nutmeg and refrigerate at least 4 hours. Serve chilled.

YIELD: 2 CUPS

CRANBERRY PRESERVES

Preserves, unlike jams or jellies, feature whole berries.

- 4 **cups sugar**
- 4 **cups water**
- 2 **pounds fresh cranberries**
  Zest of 2 oranges
  Juice of 2 limes

1. Dissolve the sugar in the water and simmer over medium heat for 10 minutes. Add the cranberries, zest, and lime juice, and increase heat to high. Stir constantly to prevent burning as you allow the syrup to thicken and reduce, about 20 minutes.

2. Distribute into sterilized jars and refrigerate for up to 2 weeks, or process in boiling water according to the manufacturer's instructions for 10 minutes (up to 1,000 feet altitude; adjust processing times for elevations over 1,000 feet).

YIELD: 10 JARS

CRANBERRY CHUTNEY

I recommend having jars of this colorful chutney ready to send home with your dinner guests! This is great with any white meat, hot or cold, and with ham or cold roast beef.

>   4 cups fresh cranberries
>   1 cup chopped Vidalia onion
>   ¾ cup fresh squeezed grapefruit juice
>   ¾ cup apple cider vinegar
>   ½ cup apple cider
>   2 teaspoons grated grapefruit zest
>   1 tablespoon minced fresh ginger
>   1 teaspoon allspice
>   1 teaspoon cinnamon
>   1 cup maple syrup
>   ½ cup brown sugar
>   1¼ cups pecans, chopped

1. Bring the cranberries, onion, juice, vinegar, cider, zest, ginger, allspice, and cinnamon to a boil.

2. Once the mixture has reached the boiling point, lower the heat and simmer for 10 minutes.

3. After 10 minutes, add the maple syrup and brown sugar, stirring. Continue to stir every few minutes for an additional 15 minutes, or until the chutney has thickened sufficiently. Stir in the pecans.

4. Remove from heat and spoon into sterilized jars. Refrigerate for up to 2 weeks, or process in boiling water according to the manufacturer's instructions for 10 minutes (up to 1,000 feet altitude; adjust processing times for elevations over 1,000 feet).

YIELD: 5 JARS

Chutney Hint

If you forget to stir a sugary batch, the bottom of the pan may scorch and create a layer of burned chutney. Refrain from scraping the burned bits up into the rest of the batch, or you'll spoil it. When you jar the chutney, take great care that you don't dislodge the burned parts. Tilt the pan and scoop from the chutney that slides to the sides of the pan. Sacrifice the layer of "good" chutney that doesn't slide.

CRANBERRY JELLY

For a tangy twist to the old peanut butter and jelly sandwich, try this jazzy delight.

8 cups fresh cranberries
5 cups water
5 cups sugar
3 ounces liquid pectin

1. Simmer the cranberries in the water, covered, over medium heat for 15 minutes. Strain the cranberry mixture through a sieve, and measure 6 cups of the pulp/juice that results.

2. Place the juice in a heavy-bottomed cooking pot over medium-high heat. Add the sugar, stirring well, and bring to a boil. Add the pectin and boil for 1 minute.

3. Remove from the heat and, with a slotted or mesh spoon, skim off the foam. Pour into hot sterilized jars and refrigerate for up to 2 weeks, or process in boiling water according to the manufacturer's directions for 10 minutes (up to 1,000 feet altitude; adjust processing times for elevations over 1,000 feet).

YIELD: 10 JARS

Sweets and Treats

These desserts — some traditional favorites, plus a few that I've discovered along the way — are some of the best around. Several are great for storing or transporting if you want to share . . . but who will be the wiser if you don't?

THE BEST CHOCOLATE CHIP COOKIE

The contrast of the tangy cranberries with the sweet chunks of chocolate in these cookies is delightful. When made with dried cranberries, the cookies are a bit sweeter.

    8 tablespoons butter, softened
    ¼ cup granulated sugar
    ⅓ cup light brown sugar, firmly packed
    1 large egg
    ½ teaspoon pure vanilla extract
    1 cup plus 2 tablespoons all-purpose flour
    ½ teaspoon baking soda
 1½ cups fresh chopped cranberries or 1 cup dried cranberries
    1 cup semisweet chocolate chips
    ½ cup walnuts, chopped

1. Preheat oven to 375°F. Beat the butter and the granulated and brown sugars in an electric mixer until light and fluffy. Add the egg and vanilla and mix well, scraping the sides of the bowl with a rubber spatula.

2. In a separate bowl, mix the flour and baking soda with a whisk or fork until well blended. Add to the butter mixture slowly, scraping sides of the bowl. Mix well. When all of the flour mixture has been added, remove and scrape beaters.

3. Add the cranberries, chocolate chips, and walnuts to the dough and stir in carefully. Spoon onto ungreased baking sheets, in tablespoon-sized dollops about 2 inches apart. Bake for 20 minutes, rotating the baking sheets in the oven every 5 minutes to ensure even baking. Let cool on the sheets for a few minutes before transferring to wire racks for complete cooling.

YIELD: 2½ DOZEN

CRANBERRY–GINGER PINWHEELS

These are festive, impressive, and easy to transport — a great gift cookie.

- ¾ cup whole-berry cranberry sauce (canned is fine)
- ¼ cup ginger preserves
- 1 tablespoon cornstarch
- ¾ cup brown sugar, firmly packed
- ½ cup (1 stick) butter, softened
- 1 egg
- 1¾ cups all-purpose flour
- 1 teaspoon baking powder
- ¼ teaspoon ground allspice
- ¼ teaspoon ground nutmeg
- ¼ teaspoon salt

1. To make the filling, over medium-high heat, bring the cranberry sauce, ginger preserves, and cornstarch to a boil, stirring constantly, then refrigerate.

2. To make the dough, use an electric mixer to cream the brown sugar and butter. Add the egg and beat until light.

3. In a separate bowl, mix the flour, baking powder, allspice, nutmeg, and salt. Add these slowly to the brown sugar mixture, ½ cup at a time, scraping the sides of the bowl with a rubber spatula. Refrigerate the entire bowl, covered, for 1 hour.

4. On a floured work surface, press or roll the chilled dough into a rectangle, about 16 inches by 8 inches. Spread the chilled cranberry filling uniformly over the dough, leaving clear a ½-inch strip on each long side.

5. Roll from the long side of the rectangle, slowly and carefully so you do not press out the filling. Cut the roll in half and wrap the two rolls in plastic wrap. Refrigerate for at least 2 hours or up to 1 day; the rolls may also be frozen for up to 3 months.

6. Preheat oven to 375°F and grease several baking sheets. Slice the rolls into ½-inch-thick pinwheels and place about 2 inches apart on the prepared sheets. Bake for 9–12 minutes, or until golden brown, then transfer to a rack to cool completely.

Yield: 3 dozen

CRANBERRY–BLUEBERRY PIE

You can make this yummy pie any time of year, because frozen berries work as well as fresh. Ginger ice cream makes a delicious complement.

Pie Crust

⅔ cup (about 1¼ stick) cold butter
2 cups all-purpose flour
1 teaspoon salt
Ice water

Filling

1 pound fresh or frozen blueberries
2 cups fresh or frozen cranberries
2 cups sugar
3 tablespoons cornstarch
2 tablespoons lemon juice
1 tablespoon all-purpose flour
1 teaspoon ground cinnamon
1 teaspoon ground nutmeg

1. To make the pie crust, mix the flour and salt. Use a pastry blender or fork to cut the butter into the flour mixture until crumbly.

2. Sprinkle the ice water into the flour mixture and use a fork to toss (do not mash). Add just enough water that the dough forms a rough ball when you press it together, about 5–7 tablespoons. If the dough is too sticky it will be tough; if too dry, it will be very hard to handle.

3. Flour a countertop and a rolling pin. Divide the dough into two balls and set one aside. Press the ball of dough flat from the center on the countertop and begin to roll out gently from the center with the rolling pin. If the top of the dough becomes sticky, dust with flour to keep the rolling pin from pulling up dough. Roll out to approximately 11 inches in diameter. To transfer to a 9-inch pie dish, bring up one edge of the circle over the rolling pin and begin to slowly roll toward the center of the circle, lifting the crust off the counter as you go. If the dough sticks, loosen gently with a knife or scraper. Continue to roll and lift the dough off the counter, and allow it to hang from the rolling pin as you transfer it to the pan. Then simply roll it onto the pie dish and ease into place. Roll out the top crust from the other ball of dough.

4. To make the filling, combine all of the filling ingredients in a saucepan. Bring to a boil over medium-high heat, stirring constantly to prevent scorching, then reduce heat to medium-low. Stir every

minute or so, until the skins of the cranberries burst and the volume of the mixture reduces by one quarter. Let cool for 30 minutes. Preheat oven to 425°F.

5. To assemble the pie, prepare top crust by cutting it into ½-inch strips. Once the filling has cooled somewhat, pour it into the prepared shell. Arrange strips of pastry in a lattice pattern over the top of the pie, then fold up edges of the bottom crust and press down with a fork to finish.

6. Bake for 25–35 minutes, or until the top crust is golden brown. Cool for at least a few hours before serving.

YIELD: 8 SERVINGS

ROGERS RELISH TART

Here's a neat twist on my family's favorite relish, frozen for a cool summer dessert or snack.

> 1¼ cups Rogers Family Cranberry Relish (see page 19) or
> 10-ounce package cranberry-orange relish
> 1 can (14 ounces) sweetened condensed milk
> 1 cup frozen whipped topping, thawed
> 1 nine-inch prebaked pie shell
> 1 orange, thinly sliced, to garnish

1. Mix the relish with the condensed milk. Using a rubber spatula, fold in the whipped topping. Pour into the pie shell and smooth top gently with the spatula.

2. Freeze overnight; garnish with orange slices.

YIELD: 12 SERVINGS

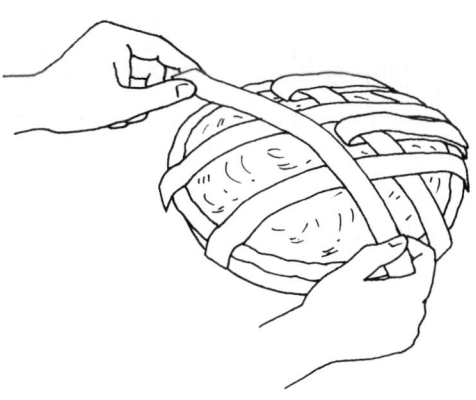

POLENTA–CRANBERRY CAKE

This Italian sweet brings the hearty corn of polenta to the dessert table for a smooth and surprisingly delicate treat. Try serving this with a warmed cranberry conserve and a sprig of mint.

    4 packages active dry yeast (1 ounce total)
    2 tablespoons warm water
 1¾ cups all-purpose flour
 1⅓ cups dried cranberries
    2 tablespoons brandy
    2 cups yellow cornmeal
  ¾ cup sugar
  ¼ teaspoon salt
 1⅓ cups chopped dried Calimyrna figs
    2 apples, peeled, cored, and chopped
  ⅔ cup freshly squeezed lime juice
    1 cup water, 98°F
    4 tablespoons unsalted butter, melted
    2 tablespoons extra-virgin olive oil
    1 egg, beaten

1. Butter a 10-inch round pan and dust with cornmeal.

2. In a small bowl, dissolve the yeast in the 2 tablespoons of water. Measure 2 tablespoons of the flour into the yeast mixture. Using a wire whisk, blend well to make a paste. Cover with plastic wrap and set in a warm place for 30 minutes.

3. In another small bowl, let the cranberries soak in the brandy and set aside, stirring occasionally.

4. Stir to combine the remaining flour and the cornmeal, sugar, and salt in the large bowl of an electric mixer. Add the cranberries and brandy, figs, apples, and lime juice. Using the dough hook, mix the batter, scraping the sides diligently with a rubber spatula. Add the water, butter, olive oil, and yeast mixture, which should have a spongy consistency. Mix thoroughly.

5. Turn the batter onto a lightly floured work surface and knead for a few minutes until the dough is smooth and elastic. Transfer the dough to the prepared pan and cover with a clean dish towel. Let rise in a warm, draft-free spot for 1–2 hours, or until the dough has reached the top of the pan.

6. Heat the oven to 375°F. With a pastry brush, coat the top of the cake lightly with the egg. Bake for 50 minutes, or until a tester inserted in the center comes out clean. Cool in the pan for 15 minutes, then invert and gently lift the pan off the cake. Turn right-side up on a wire rack. Cool completely.

YIELD: 12 SERVINGS

CRANBERRY–PEAR CRISP

One of my favorite twists on the traditional crisp-style dish, this recipe is guaranteed to turn heads. Serve with vanilla ice cream for a mouthwatering combination.

Filling
> 5 cups sliced, peeled pears (canned are fine if they are well drained)
> 1½ cups fresh or frozen whole cranberries
> ¾ cup firmly packed brown sugar
> 2 tablespoons all-purpose flour
> 2 teaspoons orange zest
> 1 teaspoon ground nutmeg

Topping
> 1 cup rolled oats (not instant oatmeal)
> ¾ cup firmly packed brown sugar
> ½ cup all-purpose flour
> 1 teaspoon ground cinnamon
> ½ cup butter (1 stick), melted

1. Preheat oven to 375°F. To make the filling, place the pears and cranberries in an 8- x 8-inch baking pan, distributing evenly.

2. In a separate bowl, mix the sugar, flour, zest, and nutmeg, and sprinkle over the fruit. Shake the pan a few times to let the mixture settle in.

3. To make the topping, mix the oats, sugar, flour, and cinnamon. Continue stirring as you drizzle in the butter. Sprinkle the topping evenly over the fruit.

4. Bake, covered, for 15 minutes. Uncover and bake 10–20 minutes longer, until the topping is crisp and the fruit is bubbling. Serve warm.

YIELD: 6 GENEROUS SERVINGS

MINI CRANBERRY CHEESCAKES

Make these impressive little snacks for a potluck or a dinner party, and they will go fast!

Cheesecakes
- 1 cup graham cracker crumbs (about 15 crackers)
- 4 tablespoons butter, melted
- ¼ teaspoon ground allspice
- ¼ teaspoon ground nutmeg
- 8 ounces cream cheese, softened
- ⅓ cup sugar
- 1 large egg
- 2 tablespoons sour cream
- 1 tablespoon freshly squeezed lemon juice
- ½ teaspoon pure vanilla extract

Topping
- ¼ cup water
- ⅓ cup sugar
- 1 cup fresh or frozen cranberries
- 2½ teaspoons cornstarch

1. Preheat oven to 375°F. To make the cheesecakes, combine the graham cracker crumbs, butter, allspice, and nutmeg in a bowl and stir well. Distribute evenly between two 1-dozen capacity mini-muffin pans, and press into the bottom and sides of depressions to create shells. Refrigerate.

2. In the large bowl of an electric mixer, beat the softened cream cheese with the sugar until smooth, then add the egg, sour cream, lemon juice, and vanilla, and beat well, scraping the sides of the bowl with a rubber spatula as it turns.

3. Spoon the cream cheese filling into the graham cracker shells or pipe in with a pastry bag. Bake the cheesecakes for 10 minutes, switching the positions of the pans after 5 minutes. Turn off the oven and open the door, but do not remove the pans. This allows the cakes to cool slowly so that the tops do not split. After 30 minutes, remove from oven and let cool completely in pans.

4. To prepare the topping, whisk the water, sugar, cranberries, and cornstarch in a heavy-bottomed saucepan over medium-high heat. Bring to a boil, stirring constantly. Reduce heat to low and simmer for 1 minute, whisking intermittently. Set aside to cool.

5. Once the cheesecakes and topping have cooled, carefully remove the cakes from the pans and spoon the topping onto the center of each, distributing cranberries evenly. Cover and store in the refrigerator, taking care that the wrap does not cling to the topping and pull it off.

YIELD: 24 CHEESECAKES

CRANBERRY–LEMON POUND CAKE

This cake is splendid with a cup of tea on a winter afternoon.

2¾ cups sugar
1½ cups (3 sticks) butter, softened
1 teaspoon lemon zest
1 teaspoon pure vanilla extract
½ teaspoon lemon extract
6 eggs
3 cups all-purpose flour
1 teaspoon baking soda
½ teaspoon salt
8 ounces sour cream
1½ cups fresh cranberries, chopped

1. Preheat oven to 350°F. Grease and lightly flour a 10-inch Bundt pan or a 9-inch tube pan.

2. Using an electric mixer, beat the sugar and butter in a large bowl until light and fluffy. Add the lemon zest and the vanilla and lemon extracts, then add the eggs one at a time, continuing to beat thoroughly between additions and scraping the sides of the bowl with a rubber spatula.

3. In a separate bowl, mix the flour, baking soda, and salt. With the electric mixer running, add to the egg mixture ½ cup of the flour mixture alternately with 1 ounce of the sour cream. Scrape the sides of the bowl frequently. Mix well to combine, then remove the beaters.

4. Fold in the cranberries and pour the batter into the prepared baking pan.

5. Bake for 1–1¼ hours, or until a toothpick inserted in the center comes out clean. Allow to cool for 15 minutes, then remove from the pan to cool completely.

YIELD: 12–14 SERVINGS

CRANBERRY-CREAM SWIRL

This moist cake makes a nice holiday dessert.

  2 packages (3 ounces each) cream cheese
  2 eggs
  2 cups all-purpose flour
  1 cup sugar
  1½ teaspoons baking powder
  ½ teaspoon baking soda
  ½ teaspoon ground cinnamon
  ½ teaspoon ground nutmeg
  ½ teaspoon salt
  ½ cup apple cider
  ¼ cup apple brandy
  4 tablespoons (½ stick) butter, melted
  1½ cups fresh cranberries, halved
  ¾ cup pecans or walnuts, chopped

1. Leaving the cream cheese in its foil packaging, place in a bowl of hot water for 10 minutes to soften. Preheat oven to 350°F, and grease and lightly flour a 9- x 5-inch loaf pan.

2. Remove the softened cream cheese from the foil and place in a glass bowl. With an electric mixer, beat the cream cheese until light and fluffy. Add 1 of the eggs, and beat until well incorporated.

3. In a large bowl, combine the flour, sugar, baking powder, baking soda, cinnamon, nutmeg, and salt.

4. In a separate bowl, beat together the remaining 1 egg and the cider, brandy, and butter with a fork. Add to the flour mixture. Fold in the cranberries and nuts.

5. Scoop half of the cranberry batter into the prepared baking pan and pour the cream cheese mixture over the batter, distributing it evenly with a rubber spatula. Wash the spatula, then use it to distribute the rest of the cranberry batter over the cream cheese mixture.

6. Bake for 1–1¼ hours, or until top surface is springy and a tester inserted in the center comes out clean. Cool for 15 minutes, then turn the pan upside down and gently remove it. Leave the cake upside down until completely cool, then wrap in plastic and refrigerate.

YIELD: ONE LOAF

FRUITED CRANBERRY GELATIN

This is an easy dessert to prepare for guests, and it can be chilled in individual dishes or set in a decorative mold. Serve individual dishes with whipped cream and a fan of thinly sliced fresh peach as garnish.

- **1 package (about 2¼ ounces) orange-flavored gelatin**
- **1 cup boiling apple cider**
- **1 cup chopped peach**
- **½ cup sugar**
- **2 cups fresh cranberries**

1. Dissolve the gelatin in the apple cider, then pour into a blender or food processor.

2. Add the peach and sugar and blend well, then turn speed to high and add the cranberries a few at a time, until the mixture becomes thick enough that the top layer does not move.

3. Pour or spoon into a mold or individual dessert cups and refrigerate to set. Individual dishes will be ready within an hour; molds should set for at least 2 hours, depending on dimensions.

YIELD: 6 SERVINGS

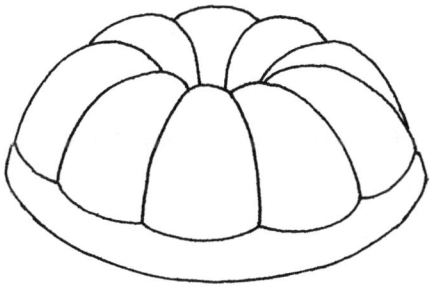

Resources

Cape Cod Cranberry Growers' Association
508-866-7878
www.cranberries.org

Cranberry Hill Farm
508-888-9179
www.localharvest.org/cranberry-hill-organic-farm-M555

The Cranberry Institute
508-866-1118
www.cranberryinstitute.org

Ocean Spray Cranberries, Inc.
800-662-3263
www.oceanspray.com

Wisconsin State Cranberry Growers Association
715-423-2070
www.wiscran.org